Thomas Jefferson

by Judy Emerson

Consulting Editor: Gail Saunders-Smith, Ph.D.

Pebble Books

an imprint of Capstone Press
Mankato, Minnesota

Pebble Books are published by Capstone Press
151 Good Counsel Drive, P.O. Box 669, Mankato, Minnesota 56002
http://www.capstone-press.com

1 2 3 4 5 6 08 07 06 05 04 03

Library of Congress Cataloging-in-Publication Data
Emerson, Judy.
     Thomas Jefferson / by Judy Emerson.
     p. cm.—(First biographies)
     Summary: Simple text and photographs introduce the life of Thomas Jefferson.
     Includes bibliographical references and index.
     ISBN 0-7368-2088-4 (hardcover)
     1. Jefferson, Thomas, 1743–1826—Juvenile literature. 2. Presidents—
United States—Biography—Juvenile literature. [1. Jefferson, Thomas, 1743–1826.
2. Presidents.] I. Title. II. First biographies (Mankato, Minn.)
E332.79 .E56 2004
973.4′6′092—dc21   2002155691

Pebble Books thanks Robin Gabriel, the Director of
Education at Monticello/Thomas Jefferson Foundation,
Charlottesville, Virginia, for consulting on this book.

Note to Parents and Teachers

The First Biographies series supports national history standards for
units on people and culture. This book describes and illustrates the
life of Thomas Jefferson. The photographs support early readers in
understanding the text. This book also introduces early readers to
subject-specific vocabulary words, which are defined in the Words
to Know section. Early readers may need assistance to read some
words and to use the Table of Contents, Words to Know, Read
More, Internet Sites, and Index/Word List sections of the book.

Table of Contents

Time Line

1743
born

Thomas Jefferson was born in 1743 in Virginia. Virginia was a British colony. Thomas grew up on a farm. He read many books.

Time Line

1743
born

1767
becomes
a lawyer

Thomas became a lawyer in 1767. He was a great thinker and writer. Thomas wrote about the rights of the colonists.

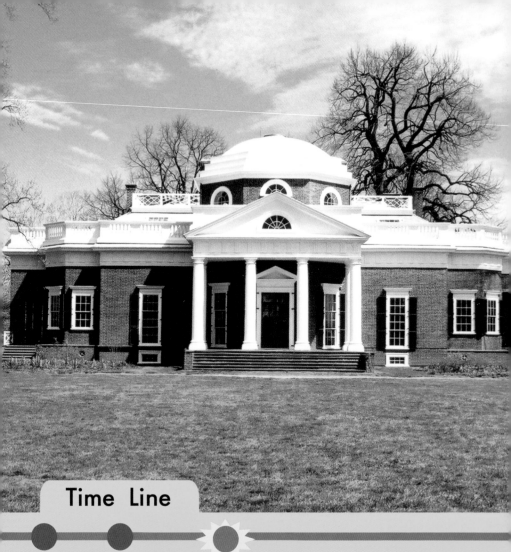

Time Line

1743
born

1767
becomes
a lawyer

1772
marries Martha
Wayles Skelton

Thomas married Martha Wayles Skelton in 1772. They lived on a plantation called Monticello. Slaves lived and worked on the large farm.

Today, Monticello is a museum for visitors.

Time Line

1743
born

1767
becomes
a lawyer

1772
marries Martha
Wayles Skelton

1776
writes Declaration
of Independence

Thomas wrote the Declaration of Independence in 1776. This paper said the colonies were free from Great Britain. Colonists wanted to make their own laws.

Time Line

1743	1767	1772	1776
born	becomes a lawyer	marries Martha Wayles Skelton	writes Declaration of Independence

The colonists fought Great Britain in the Revolutionary War. The colonists won the war in 1783. They formed a new country called the United States of America.

Time Line

1743
born

1767
becomes
a lawyer

1772
marries Martha
Wayles Skelton

1776
writes Declaration
of Independence

Thomas helped the new country form its government. In 1801, Thomas became the third president of the United States.

1801
becomes third
president

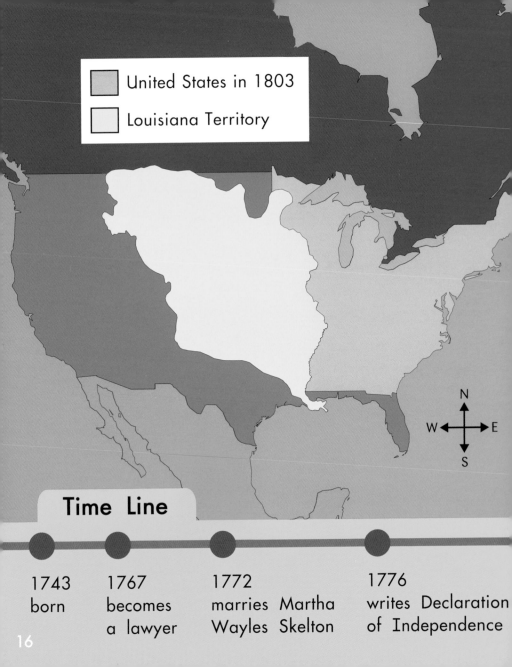

United States in 1803

Louisiana Territory

N
W — E
S

Time Line

1743 born	1767 becomes a lawyer	1772 marries Martha Wayles Skelton	1776 writes Declaration of Independence

As president, Thomas helped the United States buy the Louisiana Territory from France. This land doubled the size of the United States.

1801
becomes third
president

1803
helps buy
Louisiana
Territory

Time Line

1743
born

1767
becomes
a lawyer

1772
marries Martha
Wayles Skelton

1776
writes Declaration
of Independence

In 1809, Thomas went home to Virginia. He helped plan and build the University of Virginia. He also gave advice to other presidents.

◄ the University of Virginia, around 1830

1801
becomes third
president

1803
helps buy
Louisiana
Territory

1809
returns to
Monticello

Time Line

1743
born

1767
becomes
a lawyer

1772
marries Martha
Wayles Skelton

1776
writes Declaration
of Independence

Thomas Jefferson died in 1826. Americans remember him as the "Father of the Declaration of Independence."

1801
becomes third president

1803
helps buy Louisiana Territory

1809
returns to Monticello

1826
dies

Words to Know

advice—an idea or suggestion about what to do

colonist—a person who lives in a colony

colony—an area that is settled by people from another country and that is ruled by that country

declaration—an important announcement

government—the people who rule a country

independence—freedom; independent people make decisions for themselves.

lawyer—a person who is trained to help people with the law

plantation—a large farm where one main crop is grown; slaves lived on some plantations.

Revolutionary War—the war in which the 13 American colonies won their freedom from Great Britain; this war lasted from 1775 to 1783.

slave—someone who is owned by another person; slaves are not free to choose their homes or jobs.

territory—a large area of land; the United States bought the Louisiana Territory from France for about $15 million.

Read More

Frost, Helen. *Independence Day.* National Holidays. Mankato, Minn.: Pebble Books, 2000.

Murphy, Frank. *Thomas Jefferson's Feast.* Step into Reading. New York: Random House, 2003.

Raatma, Lucia. *Thomas Jefferson.* Compass Point Early Biographies. Minneapolis: Compass Point Books, 2001.

Internet Sites

Do you want to find out more about Thomas Jefferson? Let FactHound, our fact-finding hound dog, do the research for you.

Here's how:

1) Visit *http://www.facthound.com*

2) Type in the **Book ID** number: **0736820884**

3) Click on **FETCH IT**.

FactHound will fetch Internet sites picked by our editors just for you!

Index/Word List

born, 5
British, 5
colonist, 7, 11, 13
colony, 5, 11
Declaration of
    Independence,
    11, 21
died, 21
farm, 5, 9
government, 15
Great Britain, 11, 13
laws, 11
lawyer, 7

Louisiana Territory, 17
plantation, 9
president, 15, 17, 19
Revolutionary War, 13
rights, 7
Skelton, Martha
    Wayles, 9
slaves, 9
United States of
    America, 13, 15, 17
University of
    Virginia, 19
Virginia, 5, 19

Word Count: 198
Early-Intervention Level: 19

Editorial Credits

Martha E. H. Rustad, editor; Heather Kindseth, cover designer and illustrator; Enoch
    Peterson, production designer; Linda Clavel, illustrator; Kelly Garvin, photo
    researcher; Karen Risch, product planning editor

Photo Credits

Corbis/Burnstein Collection, 20
Getty Images/Hulton Archive, cover, 14, 18
Monticello/Thomas Jefferson Foundation, 6, 8,
North Wind Picture Archives, 1, 10, 12
Stock Montage, Inc., 4